CW00404932

GEORGE HEIRON'S SOUTHERN COLLECTION
WATERLOO to ILFRACOMBE

Bruce Murray & Kevin Robertson

© Noodle Books, Bruce Murray and Kevin Robertson 2009

ISBN 978-1-906419-12-7

First published in 2009 by Kevin Robertson under the **NOODLE BOOKS** imprint
PO Box 279 Corhampton, SOUTHAMPTON SO32 3ZX

The Publisher and Authors hereby give notice that all rights to this work are reserved.
Aside from brief passages for the purpose of review, no part of this work may be reproduced, copied by
electronic or other means, or otherwise stored in any information storage and retrieval system without
written permission from the Publisher. This includes the illustrations herein which shall remain the
copyright of the copyright holder unless otherwise stated.

www.kevinrobertsonbooks.co.uk

Printed in England by Ian Allan Printing Ltd.

Authors note; we would like to express our thanks to Barry Hooper of The Transport Treasury and, of
course, Shirley Heiron for their support and encouragement in the compilation of this book. Without their
assistance, nothing would have been possible. All of the views depicted herein are the copyright of
The Transport Treasury. www.transporttreasury.co.uk
(Where known, The Transport Treasury photo reference is included at the end of each caption.)

Front cover - 34051 'Winston Churchill' slowing on the approach to Salisbury Platform 4. (GH424)

Frontispiece - The same engine, but this time waiting to return to Waterloo. George's classic study, using
the steam and drifting smoke to advantage. (GH425)

Rear cover - 34002 'Salisbury' awaiting departure from Ilfracombe for Barnstaple. (GH405)

INTRODUCTION

I first became aware of the work of George Heiron through the 1976 Ian Allan book, *Trains to the West*. To my mind this was a volume that was different. Photographs of Western Region steam locomotives and trains as part of the landscape, rather than with the locomotive prominent, likewise from angles which, to my eye at least, depicted, a kind of image I had rarely seen before, but also one which was instantly appealing.

Amongst a myriad of other 'trivia' (and that is not in any way intended to belittle the photographer nor his book) such information as to style and content was filed away in the proverbial grey matter. Like most, I had at the time a full time job, a family and other commitments, railways were a hobby, one to be enjoyed as escapism. I could hardly have imagined the opportunity the recall of such information would have afforded me in the decades to come.

That knowledge appertaining to George's photographs first surfaced again in the early 1990s. At the time I was researching two Western Region books, *THE GWR GAS TURBINES* and *THE BADMINTON LINE*, both subsequently published by Alan Sutton. It was now that I recalled photographs of both these subjects in that 1976 book and consequently located George to ask for his assistance in my photographic quest.

The response was positive. Some of the views he provided I had seen before, others I had not and both books were indeed far richer for his assistance. What was also obvious, was that his record keeping was not the same as that of other photographers. Yes, he knew the subjects and locations, George's knowledge of the railway geography around his Somerset home was considerable, but he did not always appear to record that detail for the benefit of others. Accordingly it was often a question of trying to use background information to precisely place an image. Dates were not reported.

That is in no way to criticise his photo taking, indeed in some respects it might be easily explained. George was an accomplished artist, both with a camera and also with a brush. Accordingly his intention was to capture the image, not necessarily to record the trivial matter of date and time. To others the latter might be important, to George it appeared not.

The same would apply to his Southern Region photographs later. He chose locations where to him the railway subject merged with the overall scene, so becoming art. He also appeared to centre on just four locations, Waterloo, Clapham Junction, Salisbury and the route near to and at Ilfracombe. Because of this the very title chosen for this book may appear a misnomer, it is certainly not intended to be.

We are aware that some of George's views have been seen previously, certainly however not all have been. One, of Salisbury, has formed the basis for a painting by George. Even so this is the first time the Southern collection has been seen in almost its entirety. To be fair, there are probably 10 or so views we have excluded because of their similarity to those included, difficulty in identifying an exact location where a train is seen purely in open country, or because they do not depict the route in question. By no stretch of the imagination could we pretend 'The Golden Arrow' leaving Victoria came under 'Waterloo to Ilfracombe'.*

Additionally, many readers will be aware of our earlier black and white photographic compilation, *The Southern Railway Victoria Station - a Unique Perspective*. This showed views of the concourse rather than the trains. Its success made us realise that scenes of a similar type of, say, Waterloo, would also hopefully have an appeal. George's collection includes these and they are amongst our personal favourites. We hope you will enjoy the results.

Bearing in mind that the intended readership of this book will mostly be aware already of the locations and locomotives, we have decided to incorporate only brief caption information as an adjunct at available intervals. This way we feel the photographs can be appreciated to advantage by being reproduced as large as possible. This we are sure is what George would also have wished.

Kevin Robertson

* The views of Victoria may be seen in Issue 5 of '*The Southern Way*', published in January 2009.

Page 4 - 34100 'Appledore' at rest against the buffers. The water columns were a feature between the track at the inner platform ends as, of course were the grease and oil deposits between the rails (GH448).

Page 5 - A very 'strong' image, possibly taken as part of a series of the concourse. Morning time at Waterloo, with the departure details and destinations for the 'ACE' shown.

Pages 6 and 7– It is tempting to say that these views were taken consecutively, although this cannot be confirmed. The high angle view reveals detail otherwise visible only to those who worked in the offices behind, including the debris on top of the kiosks, probably forgotten for many years. Only one steam engine appears to be visible, 30035 on pilot duty, whilst this was also the period when tickets were checked or collected from arriving passengers. Meanwhile, in the adjacent view, two '4SUB' sets, stand silent. The use of an oil tail-lamp on an electric train will be noted.

Page 8 - Here at least we can identify the time of year, spring, judging from the April / May list of forthcoming 'Conducted Rambles'. The tea trolleys are interesting. Somewhere to place your china cup and saucer when they were empty.

Page 9 top - More refreshments and a seat for the uniformed assistant, should she have time to use it. Notice also the manikin on the edge of the 'Telegraph' advertisement above.

Page 9 bottom - The renowned clattering destination board for main line services. Nearby is the smaller notice board for Boat train departures, two entries being shown, one, possibly, for the 'Edinburgh Castle'.

Possibly Platform 4, (I am sure someone will tell us if we are wrong). We also know the time, so the view can be identified as part of the morning peak. The luggage lifts stand sentinel on each of the islands, whilst the loudspeakers may well have been blaring a tinny resonance, understood only by the announcer and railway staff themselves. Once the train was empty, a member of staff would walk from one end to the other, closing doors and, if the set was next due to travel through the wash, pushing windows up as well, not forgetting those on the opposite side. Meanwhile the Guard would check to see what items of personal property may have been forgotten or discarded. A scenario repeated countless times at Waterloo, captured here in still form, but also beautifully portrayed in the 1961 film 'Terminus' by John Schlesinger.

34037 'Clovelly' and its larger sister 35025 'Brocklebank Line' await departure. From the headcode and duty number the 'West Country' at Platform 10 is on Nine Elms duty No 32, the 8.30 a.m. to Weymouth returning with the 5.35 pm to Waterloo. One may wonder if the person alighting from the footplate on Platform 9 is in fact a railway employee, the uniform perhaps not quite right and the footwear hardly appropriate. Meanwhile the fireman appears to be watching the coupling up process. (GH420)

35030 'Elder Dempster Lines' making a spirited departure from Waterloo, with sanding in operation. The loco seen backing down on the left may well be 35025 from the previous view, in which case this will be for the 9.00 a.m. to Exeter and the time slightly before the engine's scheduled 8.20 arrival time. The foot crossings for staff will be noted, as will the continuity of the conductor rail, although naturally shielded at these points. (GH 466)

From the end of Platforms 3 and 4, 4-Sub No 4735 is entering Platform 2 with a train from the Chessington branch, complete with makeshift sun visor. Alongside it is standing room only on a 4-COR set, also arriving. Both sets are passing over Westminster Bridge Road to the accompanying roar always associated with this particular location. (GH1060)

Opposite top - A final view of Waterloo, the man on the left seemingly oblivious to the danger he has placed himself in. Possibly the least of his worries is that of a passing train as it can be seen he has his foot actually placed on the toe of the switch. By actually stepping onto the rail itself he is doing something that no experienced Southern man would ever do. From the outset, all were taught never to tread on any rail, but always to step over. This way there was less chance of stepping onto the live rail. (GH1012)

Opposite bottom - 35019 'French Line CGT' at the head of what, at first glance appear to be a scratch set of stock, bearing in mind the mixed formation at the front. It is in fact the 'Atlantic Coast Express', complete with carriage roofboards passing Clapham Junction, with the various portions for Padstow, Bude, Plymouth, Ilfracombe, Torrington, Exmouth and Sidmouth included. (GH458)

Above - BR standard design 4-EPB unit No 5333 at Clapham Junction with a Victoria bound working. (GH1014)

Overleaf - This time it is the turn of 30854 'Howard of Effingham' to be recorded passing under the signal bridge spanning the running lines. The six coach formation, a Bullied 5-car set, No 838 and loose Maunsell corridor, plus two vans are no doubt on a stopping service to Basingstoke, Salisbury, or Bournemouth. In the background a 'Pacific' is shunting stock in the vicinity of the carriage wash. (GH400)

Page 18, left - 35011 'General Steam Navigation' backing onto it's train at Salisbury, two more 'Pacifics' are also visible in the distance. To the left is the former GWR station. Notice the two fire irons sticking out of the space between the coal bunker and tender sides. Aside from the electric headcode lamps on the rear of the tender, the cowling for the coupling light, centrally placed above the horizontal top conduit, can also be seen. (GH454)

Page 18, right - This particular photograph by George was later used as the basis for a painting. Possibly taken at the same time as the previous one, it could be that it is the fireman who is caught in the process of climbing into the cab, whilst some action also appears to be taking place at the front of the engine. Railwaymen certainly needed to be nimble in their actions. (GH456)

Page 19, left - From the same vantage point, it is the turn of 35016 'Elders Fyffes' to be seen, with the signal cleared so the train must be almost ready to depart. Again, from the replenished coal supply, the engine would have just arrived on its train, although here either it was a rush job, or more likely no-one has bothered to climb onto the tender top to clear the loose lumps on the cowling and the pile in the space intended for fire-irons. Some of this will certainly be dislodged and fall as soon as speed is obtained. Notice the man and child on the left. George's deliberate inclusion of people in his views added a particular realism to his photographs. (GH457)

Page 19, right - With at least three 'Pacifics' in the distance, 30780 'Sir Persant' arrives at Salisbury on a down working. The driver can just be seen silhouetted behind the spectacle. At about the time the view was taken, circa 1948/49, this engine was allocated to Nine Elms. GH398)

This page - Slipping well at departure. 35007 'Aberdeen Commonwealth' loses its feet on departure to Waterloo. This particular engine has had some additional holes cut into the casing above the midway line which have then been plated over. Possibly this was to allow attention to leaking pipework which would otherwise have been inaccessible. (GH450)

Opposite - A more sure footed 35009 'Shaw Savill' on the up 'ACE'. The Nine Elms duty number shown will be '28', certainly not '281' as the latter applied to a local working for a 'T9' from Eastleigh'. At Salisbury there was a complete absence of point rodding and signal wires, the whole installation controlled by low pressure pneumatic means, one motor from which is visible just off the edge of the down bay. (GH452)

Devoid of movement and of people save for a solitary porter. 35009 'Shaw Savill' has a cab empty of crew, as it waits at the east end of Salisbury station. The wicker pigeon baskets were a common site at many stations, these apparently empty and probably waiting to be returned to their home stations and owners. The difference in the external casing of 35009 compared with 35022 opposite is obvious. Also, under a glass, the brake blocks can be seen to be proud of the engine wheels, although no doubt the tender hand-brake was screwed on hard. In the book of George's paintings, *PORTARITS OF STEAM* (Ian Allan), his biographer, Michael Harris, refers to George cycling 50 or so miles each way to particular locations, Salisbury being one of these. When asked why he never went to other locations, the other side of the tunnel at Salisbury for example, George's reply was simple, "Never knew about them". George recounted how there was a café under the arches beneath Salisbury station which, one day, he was frequenting with a friend. That is until the vibration of a 'Merchant Navy' above caused the ceiling to collapse whilst they were inside.(GH451)

Clearly platform end views were a favourite for George, this is just one of several from around the same point, out of which we have tried to select the very best. The engine is easily identified, 35022 'Holland America Line', from the final batch of 10 locomotives of the class, built from 1948 onwards. 35022 also has the modified wedge front to the cab and is probably sporting blue livery. Three man can be seen atop the tender, two engaged in shovelling coal forward as the engine had already worked through from Exeter on Exmouth Junction duty No 497. The train had left Exeter at 12.30 pm, arriving at Salisbury at 2.09 pm where there were just six minutes allowed before departure. Waterloo arrival time was 4.03 pm. The loco would return west in charge of the 10.15 pm goods from Nine Elms, due to arrive due at Exeter at 2.50 am. (GH462)

Opposite top - The companion view to that seen on the previous page. The driver has completed his oiling round, although the two men are still working away on the tender, one with a coal pick, the other with a shovel. The slots on the casing either side of the nameplate were the sand fillers. (GH461)

Opposite bottom - All we know of this working is that given by the 'SPL' note on the headcode disc, for whilst duty No. 101 was allocated to Feltham, it is more likely that this was a set of Nine Elms men on what could well be a relief West of England service. The engine is 34055 'Fighter Pilot', allocated to Nine Elms, Exmouth Junction, although mainly Salisbury, during the 1950's. A decade later, this engine would end its days as a stationary boiler, testing safely valves outside the front of Eastleigh Works. (GH427)

Above - A Bulleid design open saloon third, No S1501S is the first vehicle behind 34047 'Callington' as it gets away eastwards, on the up local line. The tender, whilst appearing to be well stocked, also contains a fair proportion of 'duff', which will no doubt be the cause of comment on the footplate before too long. (GH423)

Opposite top - Conversation piece alongside 34031 'Torrington', standing at Platform 1. For ten years, from 1949 to 1959, this was an Exmouth Junction engine, although the depot had only a restricted number of duties for 'West Country' class engines travelling beyond Salisbury to Waterloo. (GH416)

Opposite bottom - The unusual sight, for the Southern Region, of double heading although whether the pilot engine is being attached or detached is not clear. At this stage we expect readers to be shouting! But apart from the gradients at Folkestone Harbour, Exeter, Ilfracombe, and between Weymouth and Dorchester it was rare to see double heading apart from on the S & D and Eastern Section 'Night Ferry' workings. The combination is of 34044 'Woolacombe' and 34028 'Eddystone', both in early pseudo BR livery and retaining their original SR yellow bands. Both 34028 and 34044 would be rebuilt in later years. (GH421)

Above - 34058 'Sir Frederick Pile' on what was once a turn for a 'T9'. The duty number, a Salisbury to Eastleigh local, is probably incorrect as the headcode refers to the West of England line. (GH429)

With a casing that is definitely displaying the effect of a few years in service, 34051 'Winston Churchill' appears ready to depart. In the background the roof of the former GWR station is definitely showing signs of neglect. All passenger services had been concentrated at the former SR station at Salisbury from 1932 onwards. At this stage the former GWR site was still being used for stabling stock whilst, in more recent years and with the track removed, the main building has found a new use for a non railway related commercial enterprise. 34051 is now preserved as part of the national collection, but has not been in steam since withdrawn in September 1965. (GH426)

George's night-time photography is no less dramatic. Here he has recorded 34060 '25 Squadron' being replenished. Three ghost images can be seen, two of the fireman in separate poses, and possibly resting for a while against the skyline. The driver appears to be spending some time attending to something under the framing, perhaps pipework from the mechanical lubricator. The engine, though, seems almost ready to depart. Notice also the unattended hose from the water column, the chain for which rests against the tender side. (GH430)

Above - Appropriately, West Country 34002 'Salisbury' at Salisbury. From the number of observers it is tempting to suggest this may have been a special working, although as referred to in the introduction, we have no detail of dates. (34002 was used for several 'Farewell to Steam' runs on the leg between Waterloo and Salisbury in the summer of 1966. There is no apparent record of a special working involving the engine in the reverse direction). Notice also, when compared to the view on page 27, that the casing has been removed ahead of the cylinders. (GH410)

Right - 34014 'Budleigh Salterton' in platform 2. The turned in sides to the cab sheet afforded a cab that was generally free from drafts, although the disadvantage was that the interior would also become intolerably hot on occasions. (GH411)

Page 32, left - 35011 'General Steam Navigation' arriving at Platform 4 with the down 'ACE', although without the customary headboard. The engine will work through to Exeter although the Nine Elms crew will relieved at the station. (GH455)

Page 32, right - A final view of an up train from the vantage point of the footbridge. This is 35019 'French Line CGT', on what might well be a running in turn between Salisbury and Eastleigh following overhaul. The coal is in definite need of trimming. (Gh459)

Page 33, left - A rather grimy 35021 'New Zealand Line' just departing west with sanders on. The down main starting signal, No. 63 is in the 'Off' position with the controlling 'West' box in the distance. (GH460)

Page 33, right - This time it is the turn of 34045 'Ottery St Mary' to await departure. (GH422)

Page 34 - With returning milk empties westwards, 35010 'Blue Star' is seen at the end of the station. Upper quadrants signals had been provided during the early British Railways era. (GH453)

Above - Displaying evidence of a previous casing fire, 34027, as yet un-named, arrives from the west on an Exmouth Junction duty. (GH414)

Previous page - In the days when is was regular practice to see party reserved stickers on a Maunsell coach attached to the front of a Bulleid design set (one of your authors recalls a school trip in this fashion), 34055 'Fighter Pilot' awaits departure from Salisbury - well, as soon as the Fireman has finished on the tender at least! The leading vehicle is a Maunsell Corridor Third, the design for which dated back to 1930 and was originally intended for the Waterloo - Portsmouth services. Behind is a Bulleid 59 foot five-compartment Brake Third, part of a three coach set. 34055 looks somewhat less well groomed than when seen previously on page 24. (GH428)

Above - This time it is the turn of 35024 'East Asiatic Company', receiving assistance in the prior to setting off. This particular engine was one of a handful in the class to be withdrawn when due for a general overhaul, which accounts for the relatively short timescale between rebuilding in April 1959 and withdrawal in January 1965. (GH464)

Opposite top - This time it is the turn of 35023 'Holland Afrika Line' to be recorded west of Salisbury. Due to weight restrictions, the 'Merchant Navy' class never travelled west of Exeter whilst for the whole of the 1950s 35023 was based at Exmouth Junction and would therefore have spent 10 years shuttling between Exeter, Salisbury and Waterloo. The engine was rebuilt in February 1957, but even after this returned to Exmouth Junction, before being transferred to Bournemouth in the early part of 1960. It would survive until the end of southern steam in July 1967. (GH463)

Opposite bottom - Coincidentally, this is a view of the engine seen opposite, 35024, but in original form and displaying blue livery. Compared with the 'West Country' and 'Battle of Britain' type, the unrebuilt 'Merchant Navy' design always appeared fatter due, of course, to the larger diameter boiler. George's record of the view is between Salisbury and Yeovil Junction, (someone will of course be able to identify exactly where), but, and as mentioned in the introduction, the subject, rather then the location was more important to the photographer. (GH465)

At the same location as that portrayed in the view of 35024 on page 39, this time 30744 'Maid of Astolat' is seen. 30744 spent the last years of its life mainly around Exmouth Junction, Salisbury, Basingstoke, but with brief spells at both Feltham and Eastleigh. So many moves around system may imply that the engine was not best favoured by its owning depot. The instruction to transfer a member of a particular type of motive power was often welcomed by a shed master thus able thus to dispose of a 'lame-duck'. This, however, must be read as surmise only, as for a while also it was policy to concentrate the various sub-classes, 'Urie' and 'Maunsell' members of the 'King Arthur' class together at the same depot. The mid 1950s witnessed a general cull of the Urie 'King Arthur' type, their place being taken by new BR Standard 'Class 5's. 30744 was withdrawn in January 1956. (GH399)

Apparently the only view of a Mogul in the collection, by 'U' class 2-6-0 No 31792. Once more at the same location as on the opposite page. Until the late 1950s this was a Yeovil (72C) based engine, meaning it would have been expected to cover local workings in the Yeovil area. However, a close glimpse reveals duty No. 482 is displayed, which involved a lengthy daily working commencing (Monday's and Saturdays Excepted) at Eastleigh at 12.09 am., following which there was a period of shunting before reaching Salisbury attached to the 1.50 am working. After this it reached its home depot of Yeovil, courtesy of the 2.41 am passenger, where it was then turned and serviced ready for the remainder of the day's turn. This included the 12.48 pm Yeovil (ex Ilfracombe) to Salisbury, which it took through to Salisbury. It was then involved in a local goods turn from Salisbury East to the yard at Milford after which it returned to Salisbury, ready to haul the 7.45 pm from Cardiff to its destination at Portsmouth and Southsea. Following further servicing at Fratton, the engine would find its way to Eastleigh ready for a repeat performance. It would appear likely that what is seen here is the Yeovil to Salisbury leg of the working. Obviously a number of different loco crews were involved. (GH402)

Above - 34031 'Torrington' on what can only described as a lightweight train of four bogie vehicles and what appears to be a CCT and a milk tank at the rear. The location is again between Yeovil Junction and Salisbury. The merits of utilising such large locatives on this and even lighter trains is one which has been debated for decades. The appetite of the Bulleid breed in consuming both coal and oil, whilst at the same time involving the region in higher than normal maintenance costs well have contributed to decline the various routes west of Exeter. The scene may be attractive to the photographer, it was hardly so to the accountants. (Gh417)

Right - One of George's photographic strengths was to manage to blend the railway and in particular the train into the landscape. Nowhere is this better exemplified than in the series of views that follow, all on the Ilfracombe line with the majority in the vicinity of the Slade Reservoirs. 34066 'Spitfire' is coasting down what, according to the LSWR diagram book, was a maximum 1 in 40 gradient at this point, although other sources have quoted the incline as 1 in 36. Whichever is correct, the Ilfracombe line was a taxing route for trains in either direction with a gradient of 1 in 36 climb leaving the station to the summit at Mortehoe station. (GH435)

Page 44 - Pounding up the grade past the reservoirs, 34069 'Hawkinge' has charge of a four coach rake on the first leg of the journey east from Ilfracombe. All the coaches would appear to be Bulleid stock although the presence of roof boards on the rear three coaches does tend to imply this might well have been a through working. (GH437)

Page 45 - The same engine, 34069, as seen on the opposite page, this time heading down the bank towards its final destination. The coaching stock is a Southern region 3-coach rake of Mk1 stock, in regional green with the set number 562 displayed. This engine was one of a consecutive batch of eight members of the class never to be rebuilt. It was also one of the early casualties, being withdrawn from service in November 1963. (GH438)

Left - Sporting a cut down tender, 34002 'Salisbury descends the bank towards journeys end, on curves which varied between 15 chain to 25 chain radius, again also with Mk 1 coaching stock in tow. (GH408)

Above - This time it is the turn of 34030 'Watersmeet' to be recorded on the bank with a down working. The up line can also be seen to have been relaid with flat-bottom track, the effect of the pounding and frequent slipping on the bank meaning that the rails facing uphill would wear fastest. It is not known if the down line was ever so similarly dealt with, prior to singling and eventual closure in October 1970. (GH415)

Left - 34070 'Manston' clearly struggling on the climb. The Pacifics were allowed a maximum unassisted load of 205 tons for up trains and 240 tons for down trains. Taking the average tare weight of an empty coach of around 33 tons, a quick calculations reveals the maximum allowed for a single engine could be as low as six vehicles. (GH439)

Above - This time it is 34061, '73 Squadron' which is hard at work. For the majority of its life, 1951 to 1960, this engine was based at Exmouth Junction, before migrating to Dover. There was a brief return to the west country in 1963 before finally settling at Eastleigh in June 1964, from where it was withdrawn two months later. (GH432)

Page 50, overleaf - The 1030 am departure from Ilfracombe, better known as 'The Atlantic Coast Express', on the first leg of its journey eastwards. Arrival at Waterloo was scheduled for 3.40 pm. In charge is 34066 'Spitfire'. (GH434)

Previous page - 34086 '219 Squadron', which had two spells in the west, 1957-58 and 1962-64. It would appear that at its various depots. This was regarded as a good engine, by which would probably account for its clean livery. (GH445)

Above - By comparison with the previous image, this is a rather grimy 34075 '264 Squadron', on a featherweight train. The illustration must be post October 1957, as prior to this time, the locomotive had spent all of its time on the south-eastern section. Much has been written and will no doubt continue to be so, on the necessity of building so many large engines, destined to while away their time on trains such as this. This would not be the place to continue such discussions. Suffice to say that having a fleet of similar engines should, in theory, have enabled crews, both footplate and maintenance, to become conversant with, even if not always delighted with, their steeds. (GH440)

Above - An unidentified 'Pacific' ascending Mortehoe bank. The train consists of five Mk 1 coaches, a type which first appeared on the line in 1955.

Page 54, overleaf - 34079 '141 Squadron', for many years a Ramsgate engine, which appeared west of Exeter from February 1958 onwards. 34079 displays its ATC battery box above the buffer beam, which means it is possible to date the view as after the spring of 1959, but before subsequent transfer to Eastleigh in September 1964. (GH441)

Page 55, left - Approaching Slade Tunnel in the down direction, 34002 'Salisbury' is in charge of a three-coach BR set. (GH409)

Page 55, right - May 1964 sees 34081 '82 Squadron' on the last lap of the journey to Ilfracombe with the down 'ACE'. The service ceased from 5th September 1964. (GH444)

Page 57 - A powerful image of 34020 'Seaton' with steam to spare, as it coasts down the bank from the tunnel. Following regional boundary changes, this was one of the engines transferred to Western Region stock at the end of 1962 and a victim of the withdrawal of former SR steam stock by the WR in September 1964. (GH413)

Page 57 - Another 'Battle of Britain' pacific, this time No 34063 '229 Squadron' at Slade. It is strange to relate that a considerable number of the 'Squadron' locomotives migrated to the west, rather than identical engines named after west country locations. (GH433)

Page 58 - A decidedly filthy 'Pacific' has just emerged from the twin bores of Slade Tunnel, if it can be truly called a tunnel being just 69 yards in length. The train is bound for Barnstaple.

Page 59, top - A clean (ish) engine in the form of 34015 'Exmouth' leaves the tunnel in May 1964 with a down evening train. (GH412)

Page 59, bottom - Under the watchful eye of Shirley Heiron, 34002 'Salisbury' is at the terminus awaiting departure. Possibly there is evidence of a recent special working, as the tyres are of a lighter shade. Of course it may be that the wheelsets had been exchanged. The speedometer fitting, attached to the RNS driving wheel, was added in June 1960. (GH407)

Left - 34066 'Spitfire' struggles as it leaves the terminus and immediately commences to climb. The bracket on the left controlled the entry for down trains into platforms 1 or 2 and also the up or down sidings.(GH436)

Right - Seen from ground level, the crew (unfortunately not named) of 34002 'Salisbury' prior to departure. The engine appears to be in good external condition. The condition of the trackwork and most especially the sleepers and ballast will be noted, typical of the residue from where engines would stand awaiting departure. (GH404)

Overleaf - A wonderful portrait of 34002 'Salisbury' and 34081 '92 Squadron' filling the platforms. 34081 has been released from its train by the engine release crossover at the west end of platform 2 and will now shunt the stock before turning. (GH406)

Page 64 - 34002 'Salisbury' for the final time. A passenger joining the train here in 1964 would have a journey of 226½ miles back to Waterloo taking, at best around 5 hours 10 minutes. The only method of public transport nowadays between the two, avoiding changing, is by coach. Now the journey time is in excess of six hours. (GH407)

For those wishing to learn more concerning the Ilfracombe Branch, the following are recommended;

'The Ilfracombe Line' published by Irwell press

'Branch Line to Ilfracombe', published by Middleton Press.